To LOVE
WITH ALL YOUR
HEART

FRAN SCIACCA

NAVPRESS

BRINGING TRUTH TO LIFE

P.O. Box 35001, Colorado Springs, Colorado 80935

OUR GUARANTEE TO YOU

We believe so strongly in the message of our books that we are making this quality guarantee to you. If for any reason you are disappointed with the content of this book, return the title page to us with your name and address and we will refund to you the list price of the book. To help us serve you better, please briefly describe why you were disappointed. Mail your refund request to: NavPress, P.O. Box 35002, Colorado Springs, CO 80935.

The Navigators is an international Christian organization. Our mission is to reach, disciple, and equip people to know Christ and to make Him known through successive generations. We envision multitudes of diverse people in the United States and every other nation who have a passionate love for Christ, live a lifestyle of sharing Christ's love, and multiply spiritual laborers among those without Christ.

NavPress is the publishing ministry of The Navigators. NavPress publications help believers learn biblical truth and apply what they learn to their lives and ministries. Our mission is to stimulate spiritual formation among our readers.

Cover design by Jennifer Mahalik
Cover photo by FPG International

Some of the anecdotal illustrations in this book are true to life and are included with the permission of the persons involved. All other illustrations are composites of real situations, and any resemblance to people living or dead is coincidental.

Unless otherwise identified, all Scripture quotations in this publication are taken from the *HOLY BIBLE: NEW INTERNATIONAL VERSION* ® (NIV®). Copyright © 1973, 1978, 1984 by International Bible Society. Used by permission of Zondervan Publishing House. All rights reserved. Other versions used include the *New American Standard Bible* (NASB), © The Lockman Foundation 1960, 1962, 1963, 1968, 1971, 1973, 1975, 1977; and the *New King James Version* (NKJV), copyright © 1979, 1980, 1982, 1990, Thomas Nelson Inc., Publishers.

Printed in the United States of America

1 2 3 4 5 6 7 8 9 10 11 12 13 14 15 / 04 03 02 01 00

FOR A FREE CATALOG OF
NAVPRESS BOOKS & BIBLE STUDIES,
CALL 1-800-366-7788 (USA)
OR 1-416-499-4615 (CANADA)

For Ben and Sara

Contents

Introduction

The humorous story is told of two men sitting at the counter in a truck stop late at night, laboring to restore strength and alertness to their weary bodies so they could resume their tedious journeys to their respective homes. As they stared blankly into their diminishing coffee, one turned to the other and made a feeble attempt to strike up a conversation.

"So, where y'all from?" he asked his counter partner.

"I'm from Minnesota," came the reply with a slight Scandinavian accent.

"What y'all do?" was the stranger's next question.

"I'm a farmer," the Minnesotan responded.

"Got much land?" the other man asked.

"Well, I've got about eighty acres," he responded. "Forty with standing timber, and forty that's tillable."

After a few moments the farmer asked, "Where you from?"

"Oh, I'm from Texas," the stranger said quietly.

"What'd you do?"

"I guess you could say I'm sort of a farmer myself. I raise cattle," came the reply.

"How much land do you have?" the Minnesotan asked, following the pattern the two men had established for this late-night dialogue.

"Well," he said, laughing, "let's just say if I jumped out of bed before dawn and drove my pickup wide open all day long, when the sun set I'd be about halfway across my land," the proud Texan responded, looking off thoughtfully.

"Yeah," said the farmer, "I had a pickup like that once!"

Perspective is a powerful thing! Our perspective on something actually determines what and how we "see." Perspective shapes value systems and is one of history's driving forces. I suspect that this principle is at the core of most disagreements among people; it's also a significant contributor to misunderstandings about our relationship with God. Of course, some of our errors are insignificant and are due to immaturity. We will simply grow out of them as we grow older in our faith. But it is becoming increasingly apparent that there are other errors of spiritual perspective that we do *not* grow out of. Instead, they become the rudders of our life of faith; below the visible surface of our lives, yet influencing our vision and subsequent conduct. In fact, some are steering us adrift of the course charted in the Word of God for those who are His own.

This study is designed to be a navigational tool to chart a clearer understanding of the nature, direction, and goal of our journey in this life as disciples of Jesus Christ. It is basic in that it focuses on a neglected facet of the doctrine of salvation. It is not simplistic, however, because it will take you into very deep waters of contemplation, evaluation, and application. It will help you lay aside, hopefully forever, shallow and unfruitful perceptions of what it means to be "saved."

The apostle Paul usually divided his own books into a doctrinal section followed by a practical section. This study follows that same model. Chapters 8 through 12 build on the foundation laid in the first section as you examine what Christlikeness "looks like" in the life of someone God is conforming to the likeness of His Son.

1. THE PHARISEE

Understanding That I Can Never Be Good Before God

ABIDING PRINCIPLE   It is my *condition,* not my conduct, that keeps me from being acceptable to God. I sin because I was born a sinner.

If you would know the heart of your sin, you must know the sin of your heart. An old divine says, "You say, 'I have my faults, but at bottom I have a good heart!' Alas! It is this that deceives you, for your heart is the worst part of you."—Charles H. Spurgeon

SNAPSHOT   Of the four Gospels, only Luke's recorded a certain poignant parable about two men doing the same thing in the same place at the same time. Where they were and what they were doing is very important for us today. They were in the Jerusalem temple, as close as the typical first-century Jews could be to God Himself. And both men were praying, or so it seemed.

    Their prayers are paradigms of two contrasting perspectives on who man is before God. The importance of each man's perspective is reflected in the outcome and recorded forever as a warning to those of us who follow: one was welcomed by God, while the other was rejected. And the greatest tragedy of all is that the one who stood condemned by God left the temple confident of his approved status before God! His misunderstanding about his condition led to a mistake about his position. And in this case, it cost him his soul.

    Understanding our condition before God as human beings determines our perspective on what it takes to become a Christian, and what it means to live as one. This is no small matter. It is the single most important conclusion we can have about ourselves as Christians. It is a foundation upon which we build our faith.

Getting this right is crucial in itself. Getting it wrong could be devastating—to the point of eternal death.

So, what is your present understanding of *your* basic problem before God as a human being? Do you know? Do you think that it is what you've done *wrong*, or what you've failed to do *right* in life? Is it your sins, those words, deeds, or thoughts that are the diet of your conscience and conduct? Or could it be something more basic yet more deadly?

SCRIPTURE   Luke 18:10-14; Romans 3:9-20

STUDY QUESTIONS

1. a. Carefully read over the parable of the two temple visitors in Luke 18:10-14. What had each man obviously concluded about himself before he arrived at the temple? Explain your answers below.

Pharisee

Tax collector

b. How do you think each man arrived at his conclusion about himself?

Pharisee

Tax collector

2. The NIV's rendering of the tax collector's self-identification in verse 13, "a sinner," could more accurately be translated "the sinner." How does that change your understanding of the story?

3. *Sinner* is a pungent word, meaning "devoted to sin." Do you think the tax collector was ashamed of what he had done, or of who he was? Explain.

4. a. In contrast, which was the source of the Pharisee's pride: who he was, or what he had done and not done? (Look closely!)

    b. Which words stand out in his prayer?

5. a. Carefully read Job 25:4 and Romans 3:9-10,20. According to these verses, is man's most basic problem with God something he has done or not done, or *who he is* as a human being? Explain your answer.

    b. Why do you think this distinction is so important?

    c. Read Romans 3:5,10,20. How does God summarize our problem?

6. Consider the phrase *righteous acts* as the very best offering of our hearts we can give to God as human beings. What does God say about these righteous acts in Isaiah 64:6?

(Note: The Hebrew words translated "filthy rags" in this verse are used elsewhere in the Old Testament to refer to a used menstrual cloth. This graphic imagery revealed to Isaiah's readers how ceremonially "unclean"—and thus offensive—their best deeds were in comparison to God's standard of righteousness.)

7. Distill from each of the following verses a brief statement of what you understand to be God's standard of acceptance:

Isaiah 6:1-5

Luke 5:4-8

Romans 3:22-23

8. Now look back at Luke 18:9. Based on what you've discovered so far, why does it make sense that Jesus was so incensed with people like this Pharisee?

9. Jesus clearly declared the tax collector to be righteous. Why is this so important, considering our condition and predicament as human beings?

We sin because we are sinners. It is natural. We perform deeds of unrighteousness because they are the fruit of our unrighteousness. We are accountable to God for what we do and don't do, but more seriously, we are condemned before God for who we are. While it is true that we can make feeble attempts to improve our conduct, we cannot change our condition. Left to ourselves, we are hopelessly, helplessly, timelessly damned. This is very bad news for even the best of folks. However, it's the truth. At our best, we can be only negligibly righteous. And this is as true for the urban pimp as it is for the suburban, minivan-driving mom.

If we don't understand the "bad news" about ourselves, the good news of the gospel will be pleasant, but not life-changing and compelling. We must face the music before we can truly sing His praises!

APPLICATION QUESTIONS

10. a. In school, some teachers grade "on a curve" while others use "pass/fail." Which one of these evaluations does God employ? Explain.

b. If you had these reversed, what effect would it have on your understanding of the gospel?

c. When you think about your own relationship with God, which one of the two characterizes your thoughts?

11. a. In light of the biblical truths you've discovered in this chapter regarding the status of all people before God, how should you view yourself?

b. How should you view other believers?

c. How should you view unbelievers?

12. In the space provided or on a separate sheet of paper, write a letter to God. Summarize, in prayer form, what you have discovered about Him, yourself, and your relationship with Him. Be sure to include misconceptions that have been uncovered.

13. Think about a person or people you may have consciously or unconsciously judged as the self-righteous Pharisee did the tax collector in Luke 18. Confess this sin to God. Beginning today, pray for this person and ask God to help you see him or her the way He does.

The failure of self-righteousness—Isaiah 64:5-6
My need of God's righteousness—Romans 3:10-11

2. ADAM AND EVE

The Parents Who Gave Birth to Sin

ABIDING PRINCIPLE   If I do not understand the extent and magnitude of sin in my own life, I can never genuinely glory in the gift of God's salvation.

Sin is not doing wrong; it is wrong being—deliberate, emphatic independence of God. It is the saint, not the sinner, who knows what sin is.—Oswald Chambers

SNAPSHOT   At some point in our ancestral past, in a real garden, two real people made a joint decision to disregard the specific instruction of God. They did so in favor of the perceived opportunity to live a more privileged life "outside the lines." Though we do not know in detail what transpired immediately after their decision, I am confident that it was cataclysmic and catastrophic. The cry of death rang out for the first time. The consequences of that single choice have not only outlived the couple who made it, they have become defining constants in life as we now know it. In seeking to get outside the lines, Adam and Eve became responsible for the lines being totally redrawn for the rest of us, their offspring.

Most of us are familiar with the story of Adam and Eve. We tend to be content with an abridged version in which two naked people get kicked out of a garden, plaguing our own gardens with chickweed as a result. However, considering that the rest of Scripture is the record of God cleaning up after their one-fruit fiasco, one realizes the immensity of the choice that day in the garden.

The Fall was not small. It was the centerpiece of civilization from Genesis 3 to A.D. 30, and the half-lives of its consequences will endure to the close of human history. Understanding the fallout of the Fall is crucial to comprehending salvation, the

Christian life, and life itself. Do you realize the extent of the devastation of Genesis 3? Have you pondered the impact it has had on you personally? Do you know the difference between being "bad" and "bad off"? And do you know how "bad off" you really are?

SCRIPTURE   Genesis 3:1-13; Romans 7:14-24; 8:19-22

STUDY QUESTIONS

1. We have already seen in the first chapter that in ourselves, we are unrighteous before God because we fall short of the standard of His own glory. Just what does that mean, and what are the implications? First of all, there are serious *moral* consequences of that for us. What do the verses below indicate are the repercussions of our unrighteousness?

Romans 3:5-6

Romans 5:12

Romans 5:18

Hebrews 9:27

Revelation 20:15

2. Look back over your findings above, and write a summary of the human predicament with God. In your summary, include both the "what" and the "why."

3. There are a number of significant pragmatic consequences of the Fall as well. Being a descendant of Adam and Eve has poisoned key relationships we have as human beings. Look up the verses below and write down which relationship the passage indicates has been corrupted by sin. Then give a couple of modern examples to illustrate.

a. Deuteronomy 32:30; Isaiah 59:1-2

The Fall has corrupted our relationship with:

Examples:

b. Isaiah 24:5-6; Hosea 4:1-3

The Fall has corrupted our relationship with:

Examples:

c. Romans 7:15

The Fall has corrupted our relationship with:

Examples:

d. James 4:1-3

The Fall has corrupted our relationship with:

Examples:

---

4. Look over your responses to question 3, and then write a summary of what you have found regarding sin's impact on the relationships we have.

---

5. The reason man's relationship with himself has been so noticeably affected by sin has to do with the difference between being "bad" and "bad off." While we generally are *not* as morally "bad" as we might be, we *are* as "bad off" as we can be. Look up the verses below, and isolate the aspect of your nature that has been affected by sin in each case. Match the Scripture on the left with the appropriate statement on the right.

a. Psalm 89:48   ___ my will (ability to choose what is right and good)

b. Romans 7:15   ___ my spirit (ability to relate properly to God)

c. Romans 7:18   ___ my emotions (ability to trust my feelings; relate to others)

d. Romans 8:5-7   ___ my mind (ability to reason and trust my conclusions)

e. Ephesians 2:1   ___ my conscience (ability to distinguish right from wrong)

f. Ephesians 4:18   ___ my body (ability to resist aging, illness, pain, and death)

g. 1 Timothy 4:2   ___ my entire nature

6. Review your findings from question 5 and write a summary of the impact of sin on you as an individual. In your summary, include not only the separate "whats" but the consequences of each.

RECAP

So far, we have discovered that the Fall was a cataclysmic event that unleashed a plethora of problems and disabilities on the human race and all of creation, and that it placed each of us in a fearful place of judgment and punishment. We are unrighteous before God; every conceivable relationship we can cultivate has been tainted by sin's tentacles, and the change in human nature that accompanied Adam's sin has leaked into every fiber of our humanity. There is no place in the universe or my life that sin has not colonized.

In the second half of this chapter, you will spend time pondering and wrestling with what this means for you personally. As you read and write, be honest. Don't dodge the obvious or minimize the significant. How faithfully you *complete* this chapter will determine how meaningful the rest of this study is for you.

APPLICATION QUESTIONS

7. In the first part of this chapter, questions 1 and 2 focus on the moral consequences of our sinfulness, and questions 3 through 6 center on the impact sin has on all of life as we know it. When you hear the word *salvation,* which of these two areas do you normally think of? Why?

8. Look at question 3 on page 18. Which of those four relationships have you not seriously considered to be affected by sin before this study? Why not?

9. Look at question 5 on page 19. Which of the seven areas of your nature have you not seriously considered to be affected by sin before this study? Explain.

10. What do your responses to the previous two questions (8 and 9) reveal about your present understanding of sin?

11. What impact do you think having an anemic understanding of sin has on your perspective of what it means to be saved? (Be as thorough as possible.)

12. As a result of this chapter, has your understanding of the nature and effect of sin

☐ remained unchanged?

☐ changed slightly?

☐ changed dramatically?

Explain:

13. As a result of this chapter, has your perspective of yourself as a sinner

     ☐ remained unchanged?

     ☐ changed slightly?

     ☐ changed dramatically?

     Explain:

14. Take a moment to look over your research in this chapter. Now write down the two most important things you feel you have learned about sin and the extent of its effects.

15. Write down below the name of someone you can share these insights with. Contact that person and try to explain as thoroughly as you can what you've discovered. (Use as much Scripture from this study as possible.)

SCRIPTURE MEMORY

The extent of sin's dominion (corporate)—Genesis 6:5
The extent of sin's dominion (individual)—Romans 7:18

3. THE FOLLOWER OF CHRIST

Being Saved Has a Practical Side

ABIDING PRINCIPLE   Salvation is more than forgiveness of sin and assurance of eternal life. God wills that those He has saved spend their life cooperating with His work, and He wants to conform them to the image of His Son.

Faith makes the Christian, but love proves him. Faith believes God to be true; love proves faith to be true. —Charles Haddon Spurgeon

SNAPSHOT   The epistle of James was perhaps the first New Testament book written. Most likely it was penned during the misty years when the early believers were trying to differentiate between the Judaism of their past and the new organism Jesus called "the church" in Matthew 18. Consequently, it is a book of practical considerations that teems with pedestrian-level Christianity. The question "What does a follower of Christ look like?" finds fertile soil in its pages.

James wrote to a cadre of Jewish Christians who had exercised faith in Jesus as the Messiah. They had patiently waited nearly twenty centuries for His arrival since the promises had been given in Haran to their ancestor Abraham. Of all people, they were familiar with the need for blood sacrifices to atone for their sins. They were well acquainted with the judgments of God, having read in Scripture about the exodus from Egypt, and about what happened to the Jews until the walls of Jerusalem were rebuilt during the days of the prophet Malachi. They understood sin, righteousness, and judgment. Words like *guilty* and *forgiveness* were part of the warp and woof of their national identity.

The words of James winnowed like a refiner's fire, confronting his readers with the sobering connection between righteousness before God and life in the streets of their exile. Perhaps that is why the words of James are so important for us who live about the same distance in time from him as he did from Abraham.

In the previous two chapters, we examined sin and its consequences. We discovered that we are hopelessly bound to sin, and by ourselves we can do nothing to escape the judgment of God. The gospel is our only means of salvation.

What images come into your mind when you think of the word *salvation?* Are the phrases *inviting Jesus into your heart, accepting Christ as your Savior,* or *going to heaven* popular components of your own definition of what it means to become a follower of Christ? What's involved in being saved, anyway? More important, what's the *point* of salvation for your life *right now?*

SCRIPTURE   Philippians 2:1-13; James 2:14-26

STUDY QUESTIONS

1. Below are two groups of verses that deal with being saved. In a sentence or two, summarize the main ideas that emerge from each group. Try to connect these ideas with the specific problems sin has created that you discovered in the previous chapter.

a. Group 1: Romans 3:20-26; 5:1-2; 8:1-4; 2 Corinthians 5:21; Colossians 2:13

(Note: The verses in this group deal with what the Bible calls *justification.* Justification has two meanings. One is to officially declare or consider someone to be not guilty, but the other is even more significant: to recognize someone as *righteous*! The Greek word family related to the word for *justification* appears over forty times in the New Testament.)

b. Group 2: Philippians 3:20-21; Colossians 1:21-22; 3:4; 2 Peter 3:10-13

(Note: These verses deal with the future aspects of salvation, the final and complete purification of our souls, our bodies, and the creation itself. It is these promises that many believers refer to when they talk about heaven. This is what Paul speaks of in Romans when he uses the word *glorification.*)

2. Review your answers above and summarize what is true about people who put their faith in Jesus Christ.

3. Based on what you've discovered, do you think justification and glorification are instantaneous and final, or incremental and progressive? Explain your answer.

4. Draw a horizontal line to represent your life as a follower of Christ. Put a "J" (for justification) on your line to represent when you became a believer. Then put a "G" (glorification) at the end of your earthly life. There are actually *three* time periods in your drawing. What are they?

5. When you think of yourself as being saved, which of these three time periods do you think of? Why?

RECAP

Two promises Christians refer to when sharing the gospel are that people can be "forgiven" and they can "know for sure that they're going to heaven." We often encourage people to "invite

Jesus into their hearts" to become partakers of these promises. Consequently, when Christians talk about being "saved," they make reference only to justification (the beginning of our life in Christ) and glorification (the ending point of our earthly life). The unfortunate outcome is that the rest of our life is left out. We have some vague sense of needing to "grow" and to "follow Christ," but we believe that salvation is finished for the most part at the very beginning,

But what if *saved* is a word legitimately used to refer to everything between the "J" and "G," too? What if there are three tenses to salvation: I have been saved, I am *being* saved, and I will be saved? And what if only the first and last ones are already finished? Where should our focus be in this life?

APPLICATION QUESTIONS

6. God's intent for the period of time between the "J" and "G" on your line is the subject of this study series. It is something the New Testament writers refer to as *sanctification*. Summarize what you understood sanctification to be before you started this study. Be honest, thorough, and specific.

7. Look at your answer to question 3 on the previous page. How would you answer the same question about sanctification? Explain.

8. Paul wrote about sanctification in every letter preserved in the New Testament, though he didn't always use that word. Look up the following verses and record what each of them says or implies concerning the idea that salvation is a lifelong process:

1 Corinthians 3:10-15

_____

1 Corinthians 9:24-27

_____

Philippians 2:12-13

_____

Philippians 3:12-14

_____

9. How do the comments you read in James in the beginning of this chapter compare to what you've discovered from the passages in the previous question? (Reread James 2:14-26 if necessary.)

_____

10. Paul says in Philippians 2:12-13, "Therefore, my dear friends, as you have always obeyed—not only in my presence, but now much more in my absence—continue to *work out your salvation* with fear and trembling, for it is God who works in you to will and to act according to his good purpose" (emphasis added).

_____

a. What does Paul say *God* is doing in their hearts?

b. What does he say *they* should be doing?

c. Why does Paul's command to them make such perfect sense?

d. Why does Paul tell them to have an attitude of "fear and trembling"?

11. Write out your present understanding of what it means to be saved. Include as much of what you've learned from the first three chapters as possible.

12. What effect would focusing only on justification or glorification have on your life?

13. What effect would neglecting to focus on sanctification have on your life?

14. a. Up to this point in your Christian life, which of the three aspects of salvation (justification, sanctification, or glorification) have you thought about and talked about most?

b. What effect has this had on your spiritual growth?

c. Which aspect have you focused on least?

d. What effect has this had on your spiritual growth?

15. If you know that sanctification represents the majority of your life because it is progressive and ongoing, how should this affect the following?

My relationship with God

The way I share the gospel

The way I determine personal priorities and life goals

God's commitment to my sanctification—Philippians 2:12-13
My commitment to my sanctification—Philippians 3:13-14

4. PAUL

The Passion to Become Like Christ

ABIDING PRINCIPLE   Sanctification—to become like Christ—
is meant to be the ongoing process and passion of my life. God
initiates this work in me, and He will bring it to completion as I
cooperate with Him.

*The whole life of Christ was a cross and martyrdom; and do
you look for rest and selfish pleasure?*—Thomas à Kempis

SNAPSHOT   The final chapter of Luke's gospel records an
abbreviated peek at two disenchanted disciples who had seen the
risen Lord. After briefly listening to Jesus explain the Old Testament predictions of His entire life, their response was, "Were not
our hearts burning within us while he talked with us on the road
and opened the Scriptures to us?" (Luke 24:32). Jesus spent the
forty days following His resurrection engaged in punctuated
instruction of a wide variety of people in different places. It is
doubtful, however, that any of them received the intensity and
quality of post-resurrection teaching that was reserved for a lone
apostle named Paul.

In 2 Corinthians 12 it appears that Paul was taken up into
God's very presence and given insight and instruction so pene-
trating and rare that God had to also take special steps to prevent
him from becoming arrogant and power-hungry. In addition to
his grand revelations and visions, Paul also was entrusted with
great sufferings throughout his life. We may safely surmise from
all of this that Paul, apart from Christ Himself, is one of our best
conduits to the mind of God the Father on the subject of sanctification. It should come as no surprise that half of the New Testament occurrences of the *sanctification* word family come from
this privileged apostle.

So what does the champion of the doctrine of justification—absolute forgiveness through faith in Christ—have to say about sanctification? How did Paul view the portion of his life between justification and glorification? And how will this help us understand our own sanctification?

SCRIPTURE   Philippians 3 (read two or three times, slowly)

STUDY QUESTIONS

1. In this powerful and personally translucent passage, Paul lays out for all time the driving passions of his life as a believer. Do you sense from this passage that Paul is passive about his spiritual life because he is content knowing he is going to heaven? Why or why not?

2. Look at verses 10 and 12. Did Paul consider being saved a once-for-all thing or a lifelong process? Explain your answer.

3. a. In this chapter, Paul reveals the dual passions that are behind his every thought, word, and deed as a believer. What are they?

Passion 1 (verse 10):

Passion 2 (verse 12):

b. Read Acts 9:15-16. From this account of Paul's conversion, what do we discover would be a big part of his life?

c. How did Paul respond to this information and insight? (See Philippians 3:7,10.)

4. Paul provides an excellent measurement of Christian maturity in Philippians 3:15. Using this verse and your responses to question 3, complete the following sentence:

A mature Christian is one who . . .

5. In verse 12, Paul says, I "press on (literally: chasing on after the prize) to lay hold of that for which Christ Jesus took hold of me." He focuses all of his efforts on cooperating with God. Paul's goal as a believer was the same as God's goal for him. Then he says that the measure of maturity for *us* as believers is how closely we follow *His* example! Just what *is* God's will for us in this matter? Look up the following passages and explain what they have to say about God's will for us as believers.

Romans 8:28-29

2 Corinthians 3:17-18

1 Thessalonians 4:3a

6. God the Holy Spirit is the divine agent of our sanctification. According to the following Scripture passages, what specific role does He play in the process?

John 3:3-6

John 16:13-15

2 Corinthians 3:17-18

2 Thessalonians 2:13

7. According to the following passages, what role do *we* play in our salvation?

Ephesians 4:17-24

Philippians 2:12

2 Peter 1:3-9

8. Using what you have discovered in the chapter thus far, write a thorough definition of sanctification:

Sanctification is . . .

RECAP

Paul understood the inexpressible joy of justification, of being totally forgiven of sin and declared righteous in the eyes of a holy God. He looked forward to the thrill of a new body to complement his redeemed soul, and he eagerly awaited his eternal existence with God and the faithful saints from all ages, lands, and tongues. But he also knew that God's will for his life "in between" was that he be conformed to the image and likeness of Jesus Christ. He was confident that the Holy Spirit had wooed him to Christ, had given him new birth, and was in the process of using life in all its variegated facets to make him more like Jesus.

Consequently, Paul's two passions in life were to know Christ intimately and to cooperate with God in the process of sanctification—to lay hold of the goal for which Christ had laid hold of him. This was what it meant to be saved. Indeed, Paul saw all of life through the lenses of salvation.

9. Paul had a single goal in mind when he thought of his own sanctification. What was it? (2 Corinthians 4:8-11; Philippians 1:20)

10. What do you think this means for *your* daily life?

11. What assurance can you draw about your own sanctification from the following verses?

Ephesians 2:8-10

Philippians 1:6

Hebrews 13:20-21

12. Look back at your response to question 4 on page 33. Using your answer as a yardstick, how does your own level of maturity measure up? Explain your answer.

13. a. Review this chapter. Has your definition of *sanctification* changed? If so, how? If not, why not?

b. Ponder where you are in the process of sanctification. Is there anything that needs to change in your thoughts or actions to bring you closer to where God wants you to be? What will you do?

SCRIPTURE MEMORY

Sanctification is becoming like Christ — 2 Corinthians 3:17-18
God will complete my sanctification — Philippians 1:6

LOOKING AHEAD

So far in this study, we have seen that our major problem with God is our unrighteousness: as descendants of Adam, we fall short of the standard of God's glory simply by virtue of our humanity. As a result of our unrighteous condition, we commit acts of unrighteousness. We are guilty for what we do and condemned for what we are. Because our central problem with God involves our basic nature, we are powerless to rectify it.

We also saw that sin is a pervasive force that has infected every nook and cranny of God's creation. And it has permeated and soiled every component of our humanity. In the words of the apostle Paul, "nothing good dwells in me, that is, in my flesh" (Romans 7:18, NASB). Every relationship we seek to build is contaminated by this foul vermin. We are as "bad off" as we can possibly be, even though we are not as *evil* as we might be. God, however, in His grace, offers to us the gift of salvation as His answer to the problem of sin. He extends a once-for-all judicial forgiveness from His judgment seat of mercy because the wrath we deserve has fallen on another, His very Son. He also declares us to be righteous — as righteous as Jesus. We are acceptable in His sight, and He is not ashamed to be called our Father.

But we have also learned that God has placed His own life in us in the form of His Holy Spirit. And He has a goal in mind for each of us: namely, to gradually and permanently change us into the likeness of His Son. He wishes—indeed ordains—to make us into the very thing He already considers us to be, " righteous" in every way. Being "saved" is a lifelong process that begins with our justification and ends with our final glorification.

Our status with God is secure forever because of our justification. But our lives here are not intended to be characterized by some vague sense of "growing" as followers of Christ. Rather, we are to order our values and goals, build our relationships with others, and invest the life He has given us to "lay hold of that for which Christ Jesus has also laid hold of [us]" (Philippians 3:12; NKJV). To do otherwise is to misunderstand and misapply the grace we have received.

The first four chapters of this study were designed to lay a foundation of teaching and establish a common understanding on some key issues. In the remaining eight chapters, you will study the One into whose likeness you are being changed, in order that you might "continue to work out your salvation with fear and trembling, for it is God who works in you to will and to act according to his good purpose" (Philippians 2:12; NASB). That is, our sanctification.

5. THE BLIND MAN

Receiving Spiritual Sight

ABIDING PRINCIPLE   Becoming like Christ involves the gradual transformation of my perspective. Instead of interpreting life through my own blindness and selfishness, I receive spiritual sight and begin to see life and people as Jesus did.

Whoever sees Christ as a mirror of the Father's heart, actually walks through the world with new eyes.—Martin Luther

SNAPSHOT   In the first four chapters of this book, we have stirred up study and discussion about the subject of salvation. We have sought to replace misunderstanding about what it means to be saved with what the Scriptures actually teach regarding salvation. We also discovered the vital role that your perspective plays in arriving at biblical truth regarding God, man, sin, and salvation. *How* we see actually determines *what* we see.

In the Gospels, Jesus restored sight to many blind people. Sometimes a mere word worked the miracle; other times He employed gestures and props. For some, it was a public spectacle; for others, a private miracle. But in every case, amazement followed the healing, as a life of total darkness was replaced by one teeming with colors, shapes, and movement. I suspect it was akin to being reborn. It changed forever what these people *saw* because it enabled them actually to *see* what had been there all along. What a miracle!

On one occasion Jesus found himself within an entire crowd of blind people. But He chose to heal only one man, and then turned and rebuked the rest for being blind, almost as if it were their own fault! He declared to them that one of the reasons He came into the world was to heal people's blindness. What in the world does *seeing* have to do with being saved? Perhaps everything.

STUDY QUESTIONS

1. In the story you just read in John 9, Jesus speaks of two kinds of blindness. What are they? In your own words, describe what you think each involves.

First blindness:

Second blindness:

2. Which type of blindness do you think is more serious? Why?

3. What insight about "seeing" or understanding spiritual truth can you gain from 1 Corinthians 2:14?

4. In 2 Corinthians 5:16-17, Paul describes both a specific result of sanctification that deals with our perspective on people and a general principle about salvation. What are they?

General principle:

Result of sanctification:

5. Before Paul met the Lord on the road to Damascus (his conversion in Acts 9), he was so spiritually blind that he was bent on persecuting all the new believers in Christ. By his own admission, he did not "see" Jesus as the Messiah of His people. Look at the following verses and identify which aspect of Paul's life each one describes; then briefly explain how Paul's perspective on each aspect is being changed by his relationship with Jesus Christ:

Aspect of Paul's Life	Changed by Relationship with Christ
Acts 8:3; 9:1; 1 Thessalonians 2:17-20 (Note: "Saul" is Paul.)	
1 Corinthians 9:19-22	
2 Corinthians 12:7-10	
Philippians 1:21-26	
Philippians 3:4-9	
Philippians 4:11-13	

6. a. In your own words, summarize what you have discovered in this chapter about the way a believer will begin looking at life if he or she is truly saved (being sanctified).

b. How is this different from the way an unbeliever looks at life?

RECAP

Blindness is the inability to see what's visible, not just the inability to see. Each of us is blind to all forms of light except that which is in the visible spectrum. We've heard of ultraviolet and infrared light, but we cannot see them; we are blind to them. Jesus claimed that one of the things He came to heal was our blindness. And while it is true that He healed many people of physical blindness, He also spoke of the existence of a greater and more serious blindness: the inability to "see" life as it really is.

The apostle Paul had a profound understanding of this blindness. After finally "seeing" Jesus as the Messiah, Paul tells us that his perspective on every human being also changed. Being transformed into the likeness of Jesus Christ means that we too begin to see all of life the way He sees it. And, as it did for Paul, it revolutionizes the way we live.

APPLICATION QUESTIONS

7. Read through the following options and decide to what extent you see your life through the eyes of your relationship with God. (Check all that apply.)

□ I see being saved primarily as a private thing between me and God.
□ I see being saved as something I share with others who are also saved.
□ I see being saved as something that I express in certain environments (such as church, prayer groups, and so on).
□ I see being saved as the foundation for my life, but not something that affects my life.
□ I see being saved as a strong influence in the relationships that matter most to me.
□ I see being saved as something that leaks into every crevice of my life.

8. Which of the following do you see differently since (or because) you've been saved? (Check all that apply.)

□ success
□ homosexuality
□ compassion & mercy
□ retirement
□ ministry to others
□ spouse
□ the poor
□ career goals
□ reading habits
□ priorities
□ the environment
□ missions
□ devotional life
□ honesty
□ purity
□ money
□ contentment

□ the rich
□ sense of humor
□ death
□ AIDS
□ racism
□ children
□ sharing the gospel
□ speech
□ parenting
□ circumstances
□ ethnic groups
□ choice of entertainment
□ my past
□ politics
□ use of free time

9. Compare your answers to questions 7 and 8 above. What do you discover?

10. a. Read Isaiah 55:8-9. What is God saying here about His perspective? About our perspective?

(Note: The word translated *thought* means "plans" or "purposes"; *way* means "journey," "path," or "direction.")

His perspective:

Our perspective:

b. Why is what God is saying here so important to what you've been studying?

c. How could this passage, by itself, possibly lead to deep discouragement?

11. What encouragement can you find in the following passages regarding our *inability* to understand God's perspective?

Psalm 25:12-14

Jeremiah 33:3

12. In 1 Corinthians 2:1-16, Paul digs deeply into holy ground in regard to the process of our sanctification and what it means to see life from God's point of view. Glean as many insights as you can from this passage and record them below.

13. a. Paul said that we "have the mind of Christ." But he also clearly stated that the process of sanctification involves the "renewing of our minds" (see Romans 12:2). What can you conclude about your own sanctification in light of your answers to questions 7 through 12?

b. What needs some personal prayer, attention, and change?

14. Imagine that you died at the age of eighty. Assume that you spent the length of your days cooperating with God in His sanctification process for your life. If you could listen to the message at your funeral, what would you want to hear said about you? Contemplate this seriously, and then write your thoughts.

15. a. List one area that needs immediate prayer and effort for you to be transformed into the Christlike person God wants you to become:

b. What will you do *this week* to move in that direction?

SCRIPTURE MEMORY

Changed perspective through a renewed mind—Romans 12:2
Changed perspective on people—2 Corinthians 5:14-16

6. JOHN THE BAPTIST

He Must Increase and I Must Decrease

ABIDING PRINCIPLE   Sanctification involves a renovation of my heart. Rather than pursuing personal comfort and peace, I increasingly seek what my Incarnate Lord sought: the passion and pleasure of glorifying God the Father in and through my life.

For every sanctified man being a self-denying and a God-advancing man, his God is his center.—Simeon Ash

SNAPSHOT   The Scriptures reveal that Jesus was intensely private. He did not expose much of His own heart to people, even those who walked by His side each day. But if we are to cooperate with God in being conformed to Christ's likeness, we must receive insight about the inner passions that animated His outer world. Otherwise we will find ourselves "working out our own salvation" for mere behavioral mimicry rather than personal transformation. We also will discover that we may be laboring for all the right things for all the wrong reasons.

Fortunately, God providentially preserved an extended opportunity for us to journey into the most intimate sphere of Jesus' life—His prayers. The majority of the recorded prayers of Jesus are public prayers for others, while His private prayers are merely noted in passing. However, the gospel of John provides an exception—in fact, nearly one quarter of it (chapters 13 through 17) contains material that does not appear in any form in the other three Gospels.

This hallowed section of Scripture contains the longest and most intimate prayer of the Son of God to His Father. And nestled in this prayer is the very thing we seek: what occupied the center of the heart of the eternal Son of God.

SCRIPTURE   John 17:1-5; 2 Corinthians 5

STUDY QUESTIONS

1. Twice in the first five verses of John 17, Jesus prays for Himself. What does He ask God to do?

(Note: To *glorify* means to "honor," "extol," "magnify," or "draw attention to the splendor of something.")

Verse 1:

Verse 5:

2. In verses 1 and 4, Jesus quietly and succinctly reveals the driving motivation of His heart. What is it?

3. How comprehensive was this passion? Read the following passages and summarize what each reveals about Jesus and His desire to glorify His Father.

John 4:31-34

John 8:28-29

John 12:46-50

4. Jesus, who was "God in a body," had a clear compulsion to do His Father's will and bring Him glory. But what about those mere men who were His disciples and apostles? Did they possess the same passion? What do the following verses reveal about . . .

John the Baptist? (John 3:26-30)

(Note: The force of both verbs in verse 30 is to imply a lifestyle, not a single act.)

Paul? (Philippians 2:21-22)

James? (James 4:13-15)

Peter? (1 Peter 4:10-14)

5. Paul summarized what this meant for him in a series of statements he made to the Corinthian Christians about how his own perspective changed once he became a believer. Read 2 Corinthians 5:5-15 again.

a. What had become the new driving force in Paul's life (verse 9)?

b. How did he connect this to his understanding of what it meant to be saved (verse 15)?

6. What does 2 Corinthians 3:18 reveal about the relationship between becoming more like Christ (sanctification) and the glory of God?

(Note: The word translated *reflect* in the NIV can also be translated "beholding as in a mirror.")

7. Look back over your answers. Write a summary of what you've discovered regarding the relationship between your life as a believer in Christ and God's glory.

RECAP

Bringing honor and glory to God should be the driving force and central passion of each person who possesses a genuine relationship with God through Christ. Drawing the world's gaze away from ourselves and onto Him should be our one common passion. It inspired John the Baptist and the disciples. It is the inescapable message we learn from the life of Jesus. And we are to be continually becoming *like Him*.

Unfortunately, for many Christians today, a serious substitution has taken place. Passion for the glory of God has been replaced by a preoccupation with personal peace and happiness. God has slowly been moved from the center to the circumference. And it should come as no surprise *who* took His place!

APPLICATION QUESTIONS

8. Each of the passages below deals directly or indirectly with seeking God's glory as the driving passion of the believer. Read each reference and fill in the chart. Under the "Subject" heading, write a one- or two-word description of the area of your life that is addressed in the passage. Under the "My Happiness" heading,

write what you think it would look like to have your own sense of personal happiness and comfort at the center of your thinking. Finally, under the "God's Glory" heading, write what it means to have God's glory at the center of your thinking in this area. (Be thorough and honest!)

Subject	My Happiness	God's Glory
Luke 12:15-21		
John 12:42-43; Galatians 1:10		
1 Corinthians 6:19-20		
1 Corinthians 10:31		
2 Corinthians 4:7-11		
1 Thessalonians 5:18		
1 Peter 2:19-20		

9. Prayerfully look back over what you wrote for John 3:26-30 in question 4 on page 48, and compare your answer with your responses in the chart you just completed. Put a check by the areas of your life where your desires for personal happiness and peace have replaced a passion for God and His glory.

10. Pray over this list for a couple of days and tell God you are willing to cooperate with Him in changing these areas of your life. Ask Him to give you a desire to live in such a way that He might increase and you might decrease.

11. God promises to get us back on track (Philippians 3:15) if our desire is to lay hold of that for which He laid hold of us. If God has revealed an area of your life that needs to be recentered, commit to doing the following this coming week:

☐ Memorize a verse that deals with the area of your life you'd like to recenter.
☐ Write out the verse and put it in some conspicuous place to prompt reflection each day.
☐ Share with a trusted friend what you've learned and are seeking to do. Ask him or her to hold you accountable to do what you have determined, and ask the friend to pray for you daily for at least a month. Do the same yourself.
☐ Write a one- or two-sentence prayer that captures your desire and God's goal in this area. Pray it aloud before getting out of bed each day and before closing your eyes each night.

(Note: There is nothing special or magical about praying the same prayer; this is simply a practical and honest way to turn your heart toward the Lord before you begin and end each day, and to prayerfully reflect back on your day.)

SCRIPTURE MEMORY

Continually seeking to glorify God—1 Corinthians 10:31
What it means to glorify God—John 3:30

7. THE APPRENTICE

Valuing People Because God Does

ABIDING PRINCIPLE   If I am being sanctified, I am seeking to imitate the person of Jesus Christ. His life of humble service and sacrifice for sinful people becomes my model, my pattern, and my passion.

God gave us life to spend and not to keep.—William Barclay

SNAPSHOT   In the previous chapter we learned that the driving passion of the incarnate Son of God was the glory and honor of His Father. We also learned that we should live in such a way that He might increase and we might decrease. If the driving passion in the life of Jesus was the Father's glory, then we should be able to discern something of how He ordered His life and ministry to fulfill that goal.

Knowing that the span of His earthly ministry was only three years, Jesus would have had to prioritize what was important above what was not. Because our lifestyles are mere reflections of what we value, how we live is the clearest indicator of not only what we value, but in what order.

When we examine the life of Jesus Christ in this light, we discover that something very encouraging and yet radically challenging was at the top of His list. We need to know what it was—after all, it must be what God wants us to supremely value, too, as He conforms us to His Son's likeness. Do you have a clear picture of what Jesus valued most?

STUDY QUESTIONS

1. a. God has a lot to say about systems of values, both His and ours. Read 1 Samuel 16:7; Luke 22:25-27; and 1 Corinthians 1:25-31. What principles about God's value system can you distill from these scriptures?

b. Look carefully at Jeremiah 9:23-24 and 1 John 2:15-17. What characterizes the value system of those who are *not* being sanctified?

c. What does God say in Luke 16:15 about what you wrote in your response above?

(Note: The word translated *detestable* here means "to feel nausea because of stench.")

2. Based on what you have discovered, write a summary of what you think should be true of the value system of a person whom God is sanctifying.

3. It is obvious that God feels strongly about what His people value. And because Jesus was the perfect reflection of His Father's heart, we can discern God's supreme priority for us by examining Jesus' life. We find what was foremost in His value system in a very obscure place. Read Philippians 2:19-21 two or three times, and then answer the questions below.

a. In this passage, whose interests are made to be the same?

b. What does Paul say that Timothy was interested in?

c. What would you say Jesus is primarily interested in, based on your answers?

d. Although Paul is writing here particularly to the believers in Philippi, we can formulate some valid larger principles from this text. What can we say from this passage is Jesus' supreme value? What do you think that means practically? How did Jesus live His life to demonstrate this truth?

4. Read the following verses and explain how each supports the guiding principle that the thing Jesus Christ valued most on earth was people.

Matthew 20:25-27

Mark 10:45

_____

Luke 22:27

_____

John 21:15-17

_____

5. Read the following words from the apostle Paul, written to
believers in many different places. What do they reveal about
Paul's value system regarding people?

2 Corinthians 5:14-15

_____

2 Corinthians 7:4-7

_____

Galatians 2:10

_____

Philippians 2:1-4

Philippians 4:1

1 Thessalonians 2:6-8

6. The following passages deal with people's needs and what God has to say about them. Read each one slowly. What area of an individual's life is being addressed? How does investing in that area express that *people* are valuable?

Isaiah 58:6-11
Area of life addressed:
How it expresses value:

Matthew 25:31-45
Area of life addressed:
How it expresses value:

Romans 10:1
Area of life addressed:
How it expresses value:

Colossians 1:28
Area of life addressed:
How it expresses value:

Colossians 3:13
Area of life addressed:
How it expresses value:

7. How do the following passages support the idea that *people* should be of supreme value to those who are being sanctified?

2 Corinthians 8:12-15

Hebrews 6:10

James 1:27

1 Peter 4:10

3 John 3-4

RECAP

We tend to boast about, or at least affirm, that which we've accomplished or accumulated. And both of those commodities are the tangible reflections of what is important to us; they are the currency of our labors. But God states unequivocally that what impresses us nauseates Him! He makes it clear that what matters most to Him is *people*. And that is encouraging, because *we* are objects of His affection! However, it also stands as the sobering standard by which our own value system is measured and judged.

If we are among those who are being sanctified (Hebrews 10:14), then we must value what God values. The inescapable truth is that God supremely values people.

APPLICATION QUESTIONS

8. a. If someone were to look over your calendar, checkbook, and all the places you've driven or traveled to in the past month, what would be the top five things he or she would conclude that you value most? Be honest!

b. How do you feel about your answer in light of what you have studied in this chapter?

9. a. When you think in general terms of your own faith in Christ (what it means to be a Christian), do you tend to think of it in terms of yourself, or of others? Explain.

b. Has this changed as a result of this study? If so, how?

10. The main types of people that Jesus gave Himself to were sinners (unbelievers), the poor, the helpless, and young, growing believers. Paul followed a similar pattern. Explain *your* investment in people from the same four categories. Indicate whether you've had contact with them and how you've invested in their lives, or how you plan to *begin* investing in their lives.

Sinners (unbelievers):

The poor:

The helpless:

Young, growing believers:

---

11. Look back over your responses to questions 1 through 3 on pages 53-54. Reflecting on everything you've discovered in this chapter, where would you place your present investment in people?

Heart of stone —————————————————————Heart of God

---

12. Below is a partial list of ways to invest in other people. If you have concluded that other people have not been as important to you as they need to be, prayerfully select one idea or agency and determine to find out as much as you can about it this week, with the goal of personal involvement. (Hint: You may want to involve a friend or family member! Also, the ideas involving children are not limited to those in your own household; there are many opportunities to get involved in the lives of children.)

- Visiting the elderly at a nursing home
- Habitat for Humanity project
- Assisting a person with AIDS
- Reading to people with visual impairments
- Prison ministry—being a pen pal or visiting with inmates
- Volunteering with Salvation Army
- Volunteering at a children's hospital
- Being a foster parent
- Teaching Sunday school
- Working in the church nursery
- Baby-sitting (for free) for a young mother at church or in your neighborhood
- Volunteering at a women's shelter
- Volunteering in a soup kitchen
- Leading a Bible study
- Encouraging and helping single parents
- Counseling at a crisis pregnancy center
- Taking child out regularly just to talk
- Praying with children before bed each night
- Beginning family devotions

- Walking, running, or hiking with child
- Writing to adult child
- Writing to grandchildren
- Short-term mission trip with child
- One-on-one Bible study with child
- Including child in something on the list in question 10.

---

13. Perhaps you are already ministering to people's needs. Think of someone you could include in your involvement, with the vision of encouraging them to invest with you in the needs of others. Write that person's name below, along with what you intend to do:

SCRIPTURE MEMORY

Ministry to others is an avenue of encouragement—Isaiah 58:10-11
Ministry to others is pleasing to God—Luke 14:13-14

8. THE PETITIONER

How Sanctification Transforms the Way I Pray

ABIDING PRINCIPLE   Sanctification will certainly revolutionize my prayer life. Rather than making daily requests for my wants and needs, I discover that what I really need is a new heart. Glorifying God becomes the passion of my prayers, rather than receiving for myself.

I had rather learn what some men really judge about their own justification from their prayers than from their writings. —John Owen

SNAPSHOT   Sanctification is the essence of what God seeks to do *in us,* in order that He might work *through us.* Thus, sanctification usually involves a total transformation of whatever it touches, not a mere makeover. The Word of God teems with insights and outlooks, instructions and illustrations, commands and consolations—all pointing us toward practical, personal righteousness. In short, much of what God speaks *to* us is connected to what He seeks to do *in* us.

But how much of what we say to God is related to our sanctification? Do we view prayer as a microphone at the drive-through of life that we use to present a quick list of our needs and wants? Or is prayer a wartime walkie-talkie in the battle for the glory of God in our lives? Certainly, much of our prayer life is the product of God's sanctifying fire, but how many of our prayers focus on our sanctification itself? We may be convinced that we should talk to God, but do we really know what about?

STUDY QUESTIONS

1. Scripture records many significant prayers. Read each of the following slowly, perhaps more than once. Then summarize what is revealed in each prayer about sanctification, not merely personal needs and wants:

2 Samuel 7:18-21 (David)

Psalm 51:1-12 (David)

Matthew 6:9-13 (us)

Mark 14:32-36 (Jesus)

Acts 4:23-31 (believers)

2. Look at the following prayers from Scripture that were offered by someone who was praying for somebody else. Record as many specific things as you can that the petitioner wanted to see God accomplish in another person's life that are directly related to what you know about sanctification:

John 17:6-19 (Jesus)

John 17:20-26 (Jesus)

Ephesians 1:15-21 (Paul)

Ephesians 3:14-19 (Paul)

Philippians 1:3-6,9-11 (Paul)

Colossians 1:9-14 (Paul)

3. Biblical characters asked others to pray for them. Record all that has to do with their sanctification from the following prayers:

Ephesians 6:19-20 (Paul)

Colossians 4:2-4 (Paul)

2 Thessalonians 3:1 (Paul and companions)

Hebrews 13:18-21 (unknown)

4. The following verses on prayer have significant connections to the process of sanctification in our lives. Read each one slowly, then record the truths that relate to your present understanding of God working in you to make you more like Jesus.

Matthew 5:43-45

Romans 8:22-27

1 Thessalonians 5:16-18

James 4:1-3

James 5:16

___

1 John 5:14-15

___

RECAP

God's Word talks a lot about talking to Him—in fact, it is mentioned nearly four hundred times! And in the midst of many prayer items and themes, we discover that many of God's most faithful servants prayed the same thing for themselves that they did for others—namely, that their lives would glorify God.

They prayed about righteousness, personal holiness, and enlarging the kingdom of God. They viewed persecution, suffering, and adversity as loving tools in the hands of a sovereign God. They understood salvation to extend well beyond the boundaries of justification, focusing on this life, not just the one to come. Their understanding of sanctification not only shaped the content of their prayers, it consummated their entire prayer lives. Prayer had more to do with what God was doing *in* them than what they wanted Him to do *for them.*

APPLICATION QUESTIONS

5. Think about your own prayer life during the past few weeks. Did you pray more about what you wanted God to do *for* you or *in* you? Be honest!

___

6. When you pray for those you love, what characterizes your prayers—their needs or their sanctification? Why? Explain with examples.

7. When you think of people's needs, do you think of sanctification as one of them? Why or why not?

8. In the space below, write a prayer of your own, similar to the prayers you've studied in this chapter. Imagine that it is going to be recorded for future believers to read and study in a Bible study like this one. Make it a prayer that represents your own heart and present circumstances (that is, it is personal) but also contains the elements you've learned should characterize the petitions of those who are asking God to sanctify their own lives as well as the lives of other believers.

9. Now spend some time on your knees (alone or in a small group) and sincerely read your prayer back to God. When you finish reading, continue to pray if you feel led to do so. Spend time each day during the coming week reading your prayer back to the Lord, asking Him to make it real in your life.

SCRIPTURE MEMORY

The proper prayer focus—Matthew 6:9-10
Praying according to God's will (sanctification)—1 John 5:14-15

9. PONTIUS PILATE

What Is Truth? Does It Matter?

ABIDING PRINCIPLE   My sanctification is dependent upon the truth contained in the Scriptures. God's Word is His primary tool in teaching me truth. If I am not a student of the Scriptures, I am not growing in Christlikeness.

News may come that Truth is sick, but never that it is dead.
—William Gurnall

SNAPSHOT   One of the buzzwords of twenty-first-century journalists, educators, and sociologists is *postmodernism,* which has become a five-syllable summary of Western civilization's goodbye party for the notion of truth. Objective truths, universal truths, and even patriotic self-evident truths are no longer welcome in the world of higher education, ethics, politics, and least of all in the world of entertainment. Supposedly we have moved *beyond* the modern era, in which truth was tolerated, to a new stage in which we can construct truth as it is needed.

But the Bible tells quite a different tale, one that goes back before modern or even premodern days. Seven hundred years before Christ, there was a problem with truth. The prophet Isaiah proclaimed,

> *So justice is driven back, and righteousness stands at a distance; truth has stumbled in the streets, honesty cannot enter. Truth is nowhere to be found, and whoever shuns evil becomes a prey. The LORD looked and was displeased that there was no justice.* (Isaiah 59:14-15, emphasis added)

While this is an appalling statement, the greatest tragedy of all is that Isaiah's shocking accusation was made about God's people, *not* the pagan nation that was about to invade Israel!

The present lack of affection for truth in our generation has nothing to do with progress and modernity. It has everything to do with depravity. When Adam and Eve wondered whether God could be trusted, and then listened to Satan's accusation, "Did God really say . . . ," truth became an unwelcome intruder into the lives of those created to delight in it. Yet another travesty is that this notion of negotiating about what truth is and isn't has crept into the church. Many Christians, consciously or unconsciously, have adopted a compromising commitment to biblical truth. How about you? What is your own commitment to truth? Do you know?

SCRIPTURE   John 1:1-18; 18:28-38

STUDY QUESTIONS

1. Read John 18:38. Do you think Pilate was seriously seeking an answer to his question concerning truth? Why or why not?

2. How important do you think it is to have an answer to this question? Why?

3. What do the following passages have to say about the importance of having an answer to Pilate's question?

Jeremiah 5:1-2

2 Thessalonians 2:10

4. How might Jesus have answered Pilate's question if given the chance to respond (see John 14:6; 17:17)?

5. Read Matthew 4:1-10. What would you say was Jesus' view of Scripture as He faced temptation in the desert?

6. Look at what Jesus said to the Sadducees in Matthew 22:23-29. Considering that they were educated students of the Old Testament, and the intellectual elite of their day, why is Jesus' statement in verse 29 so significant?

7. How does John 17:17 relate to the process of sanctification in your life?

8. What do the following verses have to say about truth and Scripture?

Psalm 51:6

Psalm 119:9,24

John 4:23-24

_____

John 8:31-32

_____

John 8:44

_____

John 15:26

_____

John 17:17

RECAP

The Bible tells us that God's Word is truth, and that those who ignore or neglect it do so at great peril to themselves. It is the agent of our sanctification—the very thing that God wishes to use to conform us to the likeness of His Son.

The Word of God was the standard for the Son of God while He was on earth. He used it to combat Satan, the father of lies. He promised His followers that when He left, the Holy Spirit (of truth) would remind them of the things that He had told them, instructing them in truth. In a world where one man's lie is another man's truth, followers of Christ must know the truth, cling to it, and submit to its authority. To do anything less is not only dangerous, it's disobedience.

9. a. Ezekiel 33:31-32 contains a chilling description of the condition of God's people, a condition that was responsible for the destruction of Jerusalem and the Jews' captivity in Babylon. In your own words, describe the approach to truth that was popular among the believers referred to here.

b. If God were to describe *your* personal commitment to truth and Scripture, would it sound similar to or different from the description of His people in this passage? Be honest!

10. Read Acts 17:1-11. Both groups of people that Paul reasoned with were Jews. They heard the same message from the same messenger. However, their responses couldn't have been more different. What do you think was at the heart of each of the two responses?

Thessalonians:

Bereans:

11. What was the Bereans' commitment to truth, and how did they go about testing truth-related claims?

12. a. In what ways were the Bereans "open-minded"?

b. In what ways were they "closed-minded"?

13. The verb translated *examined* in Acts 17:11 connotes an interrogation by sifting, looking for error. It implies that this was a characteristic pattern for the Bereans. How were these Jews different from the Sadducees Jesus rebuked in question 6 on page 69? (Use your imagination. Be thorough!)

14. Below is a partial list of important issues in which a basis for truth is crucial. Consider each of them prayerfully, and honestly indicate whether you are currently more like a Sadducee (don't *really* know what the Scriptures teach) or a Berean (can turn to specific scriptures that deal with this area).

Issue	Sadducee	Berean
Salvation	☐	☐
Sanctification	☐	☐
The gospel	☐	☐
Suffering	☐	☐
Missions	☐	☐
Marriage	☐	☐
Parenting	☐	☐
Money	☐	☐
Divorce	☐	☐
Integrity	☐	☐
Holy Spirit	☐	☐
Prayer	☐	☐
Authority of the Bible	☐	☐
Sin	☐	☐
Satan	☐	☐

15. What did you discover about yourself and your own familiarity with the truth?

16. a. Review your list and examine the areas that you checked under the "Sadducee" column where you have been guided by "Christian common sense" instead of firsthand familiarity with and knowledge of the Scriptures. Select one area that you believe needs to move over to the "Berean" column, and commit to do two of the following:

☐ Pray daily that your spiritual growth in this area will increase.
☐ Locate eight to twelve verses that speak to this area, and memorize one per week for the next few months.
☐ Ask your pastor for help in locating Bible study materials that deal with this area.
☐ Attend a Sunday school class that covers this area or a related one.
☐ Find a friend, mentor, or family member and ask if he or she would like to study this subject with you for several months.

b. Call someone you know who could give you specific passages that deal with this area.

SCRIPTURE MEMORY

God's passion for truth in us—Psalm 51:6
Truth and sanctification—John 17:17

10. THE SERVANT

Liberated for a Life of Service

ABIDING PRINCIPLE   The more I become like Jesus, the more I discover that true freedom is the ability to pursue my God-given purpose to love and serve Him. Any other pursuit, no matter how appealing, is actually bondage.

To obey God is perfect liberty.—Seneca

SNAPSHOT   One of the most inviting promises to fall from the lips of our Lord was, "If you hold to my teaching, you are really my disciples. Then you will know the truth, and the truth will set you free" (John 8:31-32). Then He declared: "So if the Son sets you free, you will be free indeed" (John 8:36).

The notion of liberty has been one of the dominant themes in human history. People have struggled and died to be free of tyrants, debt, disease, discrimination, oppression, and pain. Unfortunately, as fallen human beings, we have embraced a number of mistaken definitions of what it means to be free. These errors in thinking have also penetrated God's people in significant ways. In particular, there is serious confusion regarding our responsibility to God as believers. Now that I'm forgiven, doesn't being "set free" mean that I'm free to get on with my life, to fulfill my potential as a Christian . . . with God's help, of course?

If sanctification—Christlikeness—is God's goal for my life, what can I learn about this notion of liberty from the life of Christ? He obviously was not in bondage to anything or anyone. How free did Jesus consider Himself to be in relation to the Father? And more important, how did this freedom find expression in His daily life?

STUDY QUESTIONS

1. Write your own definitions of *freedom* and *slavery*.

Freedom:

Slavery:

2. Does your definition of freedom focus on the idea of being "free to do...," "free to be...," or "free from..."? Explain your answer.

3. The following verses describe Jesus' relationship to the Father. Summarize what they reveal about Jesus.

John 5:19

John 6:38

John 7:28-29

John 8:28

_____

John 12:49-50

_____

4. Describe the image of Jesus Christ that emerges from the following passages.

_____

Luke 22:25-27

_____

Philippians 2:5-7

_____

5. a. Now thoughtfully read Luke 4:5-8 and 1 Corinthians 15:27-28. What do these passages reveal about the Son of God in relation to the Father?

_____

b. Why is this so startling, and so crucial for us to grasp?

6. a. The following verses teach an essential truth regarding freedom for those who believe in Christ. What is the only thing we are really free to do, according to these verses?

Joshua 24:15

1 Kings 18:21

2 Chronicles 12:7-8

Matthew 12:30

b. In reality, how many options are there?

7. Summarize the key idea in each of the following verses, which directly or indirectly deal with freedom in Christ.

Romans 6:16-18

Galatians 5:13

_____

1 Peter 2:16

_____

8. Review your answers to questions 6 and 7. Then read Romans 6:20-22. How does what you have learned in this study relate to your sanctification (*holiness* in verse 22)?

9. How would you change your definitions of *freedom* and *slavery* to reflect what you have discovered in this chapter?

_____

Freedom:

_____

Slavery:

_____

10. Jesus labels Satan the "father of lies" (John 8:44). What do you think are popular lies he has propagated about each of the following areas?

_____

Freedom:

Slavery:

Serving God:

RECAP

Jesus Christ promised freedom to those who acknowledge Him as Savior. Paul reaffirmed this promise with the declaration that Christ wants those He has set free to *stay* free. But he challenges our modern understanding of freedom by defining it as slavery to Christ! Furthermore, Scripture attests to this by destroying the myth of the middle ground. The truth is, we are set free to choose who will be our master! We are never free to live for ourselves. In fact, Satan has popularized the lie that we shouldn't serve anybody but ourselves, because it's too demeaning and restrictive. He woos us to be "free," knowing all the while that he is luring us back into bondage. But we are not free to decide *whether* we'll serve someone; only *whom* we will serve.

True freedom, then, is the ability to fulfill my God-given purpose as a human being: to know, love, and serve God. Anything else, regardless of its appeal, is bondage.

APPLICATION QUESTIONS

11. Describe the principle of freedom outlined in 2 Peter 2:19.

12. There are some areas of life in which, when exercising our freedom as Christians, we could actually find ourselves enslaved to sin. Look up the following verses and write out the specific areas that are mentioned. Give a real-world example of how this slavery might happen.

Areas of Life	Contemporary Examples
Psalm 19:13	
Ephesians 4:25-27	
Colossians 2:8	
1 Timothy 6:6-10	

13. Slowly read Psalms 81:10-11 and 119:45. What insight do these verses bring on the issue of freedom and slavery (especially true freedom)?

14. Review all that you have discovered about freedom and slavery in this chapter. Whose servant have you been? Be honest!

15. Scripture teaches that part of our Christian freedom is built upon accountability to one another as believers. We are not designed to be autonomous (see Matthew 18:15; Ephesians 5:21; and James 5:16). We *need* one another as we grow in our love and obedience to Christ. Is there another Christian (same gender) in your life to whom you are accountable concerning your growth in sanctification? Someone with whom you can comfortably and honestly talk and pray, especially about what you have discovered in this chapter? If so, make a commitment to do so within the next week. If you do not have a relationship like this, prayerfully consider initiating one. Each of you should have the freedom to hold the other accountable to what the Lord is teaching. This person should:

- be the same gender as you
- be accessible (in person or by phone)
- be interested in your spiritual health
- have a good working knowledge of Scripture
- be willing to make time for this

Begin by sharing what you've discovered in this study about genuine freedom, slavery, and whose servant you are. Tell the friend about specific areas of your life that you would like to bring under Christ's lordship, and ask for his or her support. Give your friend permission and freedom to check on you regularly; then be faithful to your commitment!

SCRIPTURE MEMORY

Choosing your master—Joshua 24:15
Sanctification and being God's servant—Romans 6:22

11. THE LABORER

Enlarging God's Kingdom, Not My Own

ABIDING PRINCIPLE   The rule of God in my heart means that my mission here on earth looks more and more like His. Rather than looking out for myself, I am looking to bring the good news of the gospel to the lost world all around me.

I spent my life climbing the ladder of success, only to discover it was leaning against the wrong wall!—Unknown

SNAPSHOT   For many people, life is a résumé of achievements. They study and labor to advance one accomplishment at a time along a predictable path of monetary, social, and professional growth. They tend to measure their progress by a host of socially prescribed emblems: marriage, home, cars, corporate status, and a litany of visible "toys." Unfortunately, for a growing number of believers the pursuit is the same; it is just defined differently to sound more spiritual.

Each of us is chasing something. For some, it turns out to be "the wind." For others, it is an edifice that will transcend time, an eternal treasure. Jesus spoke three times as much about this one particular pursuit than He did about His own Father! What is this profession that is supposed to fuel the passions of those who are being changed into the likeness of Christ? What are we to be "running after"? And, more important, what exactly are *you* pursuing?

STUDY QUESTIONS

1. Jesus spoke in Matthew 6:33 of two things we are supposed to continually seek. What are they?

(Note: The word translated "seek" in verse 33 is from the same word family as "run after" in verse 32.)

2. Which one of the two do you think is in Paul's mind in Philippians 2:12-13, which we looked at in chapter 3? Explain.

3. In the space below, describe what you currently understand Jesus to mean when He says you should be continually pursuing the kingdom of God.

4. Combined, the phrases *kingdom of God* and *kingdom of heaven* appear over eighty times in the first three Gospels. John only uses the phrase twice, but his use is immensely helpful as we try to construct an idea of just what is this kingdom that we're supposed to be seeking. Look up the following verses and write as much as you can glean from each about the "kingdom."

Matthew 9:35

(Note: The term *good news* means "gospel.")

John 3:1-5

John 18:35-37

Acts 20:24-25 (both verses taken together)

Acts 28:17-23

5. In your own words, explain what you understand the good news of the kingdom to be.

6. In Matthew 6:25-32, Jesus discusses our basic needs and anxieties in life. In verse 33, the word *first* denotes something primary in rank or of highest importance. With that in mind, what is Jesus commanding us to do in this verse? Explain your answer.

7. The following verses describe some of the things people tend to "run after" instead of pursuing the kingdom of God. List what people seek along with what motivates them to seek it, if that is mentioned.

What People Seek	Motivation for Seeking
Ecclesiastes 5:10	
Jeremiah 45:5	
Luke 12:15	
2 Timothy 4:3-4	
1 John 2:15-16	

8. These verses describe some of the things that God seeks. For each verse, list what He seeks and describe what is involved on your part to please Him.

What God Seeks	How I Please Him
2 Chronicles 16:9	
Isaiah 66:2	
Ezekiel 34:11-16	
Luke 19:10	
John 4:23	
James 1:19-20	

9. Review your responses to questions 7 and 8 on the previous page. Which of the two lists best characterizes what you are currently "running after"? Explain.

RECAP

For us who are being saved—that is, are being changed increasingly into the likeness of God's Son—there should be a growing similarity between the things on His heart and the things on our hearts. In particular, we should increasingly find ourselves defining our mission here on Earth more and more in terms of His mission. Jesus came to seek the lost. He desires to bring them the good news of the kingdom. God says He is seeking people who will not only worship Him the way He desires, but will stand in the gap between Him and people. The kingdom of God—the rule of God in the hearts of those He loves—is something that we should be "running after." Are we? How can we know?

APPLICATION QUESTIONS

10. In 1 Corinthians 3:5-15, Paul presents some sobering teaching regarding the lives of those who are being saved. What is the main point of each of the following verses taken from this passage?

Verse 5

Verse 8

Verse 11

Verses 12-15

11. Describe Paul's perspective on preaching the good news of the kingdom reflected in the following verses:

Acts 20:24

1 Corinthians 9:16-23

1 Corinthians 15:58

12. We have discovered that the labor we are to seek and to which we've been called is to build on the foundation of Jesus Christ. How would you rate your own "construction" in the following areas?

For whom you are building:

What you are building:

13. Describe the last time you consciously sought to share the good news of the kingdom with someone. If you have never shared the gospel, what is the reason?

14. Would you say that you are "seeking the lost" in your everyday life? Explain your answer.

15. What have you discovered as a result of this study about yourself and the command of Jesus to seek first His kingdom?

16. a. God is pleased to grant you the privilege and opportunity to share the good news of the kingdom with those who do not know Him. It is a privilege that provides the greatest joy we can experience in this life. Who are two unsaved people you can begin to pray for this week? Write their names on an index card and display it where you will see it each day. Pray for God to open a door of opportunity, and then be available and expectant as you wait on Him!

b. Perhaps you don't know *how* to share the gospel with someone, or even how to begin living in such a way that a door would open to share your faith and the good news. The *desire* to share Christ is the greatest need—the tools that you need are not difficult to acquire. Make a commitment to meet with someone who can teach you how to lead people to Christ, or attend a Sunday school or evangelism class to get yourself ready to pursue the most exciting work on earth!

SCRIPTURE MEMORY

The command to seek the kingdom—Matthew 6:33
The commitment to seek the kingdom—Acts 20:24

12. THE BLESSED

Happiness—The Fruit of Holiness

ABIDING PRINCIPLE   The person becoming like Christ discovers that true happiness is a fruit that comes from living for others and not for oneself. Happiness and fulfillment are not things we should *seek*—instead, they are what we *find* when we pursue the heart and purposes of God for our lives.

We hold these truths to be self-evident, that all men are created equal, that they are endowed by their Creator with certain unalienable Rights, that among these are Life, Liberty and the pursuit of Happiness.—Declaration of Independence

SNAPSHOT   The founders of the United States of America obviously considered the opportunity to pursue happiness a right equal to that of freedom and life itself. But the *desire* to be happy did not originate with Thomas Jefferson and those who signed the Declaration of Independence. One need only peruse the open journal of King Solomon nearly three thousand years earlier to discover the painful record of a man who sought all the right things in all the wrong places and in all the wrong ways. Oddly, though, the avenues of his journey have street names that parallel many of the roads we travel today in our own pursuit of this evasive dream and destiny.

Throughout time, people have sought to be happy. Parents wish it for their children, children wish it for themselves, and most of us envy those who seem to have found it. We struggle to define it, yet know that if it exists, it must be more substantial than cute yellow circles with smiley faces. Some of us may believe that happiness is a mirage created by empty people who don't know Christ. Yet deep within us, we believers also have memories of moments or seasons when no other word but *happy* accurately captured what life was like for us.

Is happiness really on God's agenda for those He calls His

own? Is it wrong to desire it? Or is our error in where we think happiness can be found, and how we try to get there? Most important, is our becoming like Christ the enemy or the enabler of true happiness?

SCRIPTURE   Psalm 40:1-8; Ecclesiastes 6:1-6; 12:13

STUDY QUESTIONS

1. In your own words, write a brief but thorough definition of the following kinds of people:

Blessed:

Happy:

Fulfilled:

2. The word *blessed* appears between 250 and 330 times in the Bible (depending on the version). Yet it is often difficult for us to know exactly what the word means. Sometimes it means "to speak well of" a person or a thing, but in other places it means, quite simply, "happy." In fact, the word *beatitude,* which we apply to the part of Jesus' Sermon on the Mount that begins with "Blessed are the . . .," literally means "a state of utmost bliss" and comes from a Latin word that means "to be happy"! With this insight as your starting point, look up the following verses that contain the word *blessed* and substitute the word *happy* in its place. Thoughtfully record how the Bible defines happiness, who receives it, and how it is obtained.

Job 5:17

Psalm 1

Psalm 32:1-2

Psalm 34:8

Psalm 41:1

Psalm 94:12

Proverbs 3:13

Proverbs 14:21

John 13:14-17

Acts 20:35

James 1:12

1 Peter 4:13

3. As Solomon journeyed away from God, he concluded that there is a strong connection between being happy and being fulfilled. And he unashamedly admitted that he was neither. In fact, he used the word *meaningless* thirty-five times in twelve short chapters in the book of Ecclesiastes to describe his condition and his conclusions about a life without God at the center! But Jesus—the one into whose image we are being changed by the Holy Spirit—illuminates and gives us insight into the reality of true happiness and its relationship to personal fulfillment. Look at Matthew 5:6, then answer the following questions.

a. Based on what you have discovered so far in this Bible study, what do the following words mean?

Righteousness:

Blessed:

b. What is the significance of Jesus using the verbs *hunger* and *thirst* in regard to righteousness?

c. Considering that the word *filled* means "to feed or fatten" (or "to be satisfied" in the NASB), what is Jesus saying about these people who hunger and thirst to be like Him?

d. Rewrite this verse in your own words. Include other truths you have discovered about happiness from this study.

4. Carefully review your responses to questions 1 through 3. Answer the questions below, keeping in mind what you've learned about sanctification so far:

a. Do you think that happiness is a fruit (a by-product), or can it be attained by seeking it directly? Explain your answer.

b. What insights does your answer provide concerning the happiness or unhappiness among all people? Explain.

c. What about Christians in particular? Explain.

RECAP

Scripture speaks about happiness as something that is real and attainable. It should certainly characterize those who are being changed into the likeness of Christ through the Holy Spirit. But it is clearly much deeper than a superficial "Jesus smile" that we put on as we go out into the world. We've discovered that happiness comes from ministering to the poor, enduring temptation, persevering under God's discipline, and delighting in the Word. And, of paramount importance, we've learned that true happiness comes from pursuing holiness—the likeness of Jesus. As we cooperate with God in His eternal purpose for our lives, we will find true happiness.

On the other hand, because happiness is a fruit that blooms on the tree of sanctification, we can never enjoy its sweetness by seeking it apart from God's purpose for our lives. It is as futile as searching for an apple from an oak tree. Yet if we are honest with ourselves, we must admit that we are unhappy at times. And if we are unhappy, then we most likely are seeking our fruit from all the wrong trees.

5. In Scripture, God isolates some popular dead-end pathways that promise happiness and satisfaction but lead to disillusionment and defeat. Below is a sampling of such verses. Ponder each passage carefully, then answer the questions that follow.

a. Isaiah 55:2—On which thing (acquired or desired) have you "spent money" while trying to find happiness?

(Note: Two primary vehicles we tend to rely on for satisfaction are addressed by God in this verse: what we can acquire [spend] and what we can do [labor].)

Which labor (such as involvement, ministry, or activity) do you pursue in an attempt to find fulfillment?

b. Jeremiah 2:13—According to this verse, what were God's people trying to do?

(Note: Cisterns were receptacles carved out of rock that collected water from an external spring or from rainfall. They were a necessity in Palestine because of the lengthy dry season, and could even have been called the life source for a family, town, or city.)

c. Jeremiah 10:1-5—Can you think of any "scarecrows"— such as projects, organizations, or achievements—that you are depending on to protect your "melon patch"? Explain.

(Note: In this passage, God addresses the folly of trying to derive a sense of security, fulfillment, or happiness from anything we've accomplished ourselves.)

6. a. Look back at Isaiah 55:2-3. List all the verbs in this passage that are commands.

b. What is the obvious truth here about the best way to care for your inmost self (your "soul")?

7. a. Considering that God is addressing in this passage the need for fulfillment (happiness) as well as His people's attempts to secure it on their own, what He has to say is very significant. Review your responses to questions 5 and 6 above, and then honestly answer the following questions.

b. What is my natural tendency in regard to happiness?

c. How does this display itself in my life?

d. What is God's prescription for me to find fulfillment and avoid disillusionment?

8. In the previous chapter, you studied seeking God's kingdom as commanded in Matthew 6:33. Read Matthew 6:31-32. If one thing pagans "run after" is happiness, what is God saying in Matthew 6:31-33 regarding:

God's desire for you?

The recipe for lasting happiness?

---

9. What specific truths have you learned in this chapter regarding the relationship between sanctification (becoming like Christ) and true happiness?

---

10. a. Look at the list of statements below. Check all that describe your own pursuit of happiness at present:

☐ I am happy.
☐ I am not happy.
☐ I am seeking happiness in what I can accomplish.
☐ I am seeking happiness in what I can acquire.
☐ I am seeking happiness from what I am able to do.
☐ I am seeking happiness in relationships I have or want.
☐ I look to people more than Scripture for my security.
☐ I look to Scripture more than people for my security.
☐ I think (or thought) sanctification and happiness are unrelated.

---

b. Each day this week, read and meditate on the verses that you studied in question 2 of this chapter. When someone asks, "How are you?" *choose* to answer with the word *blessed* each time. See if you notice any changes in your thinking as a result of changes in your speaking.

SCRIPTURE MEMORY

The recipe for fleeting happiness—Jeremiah 2:13
The recipe for lasting happiness—Matthew 5:6